IMAGES
of America

LEMHI COUNTY

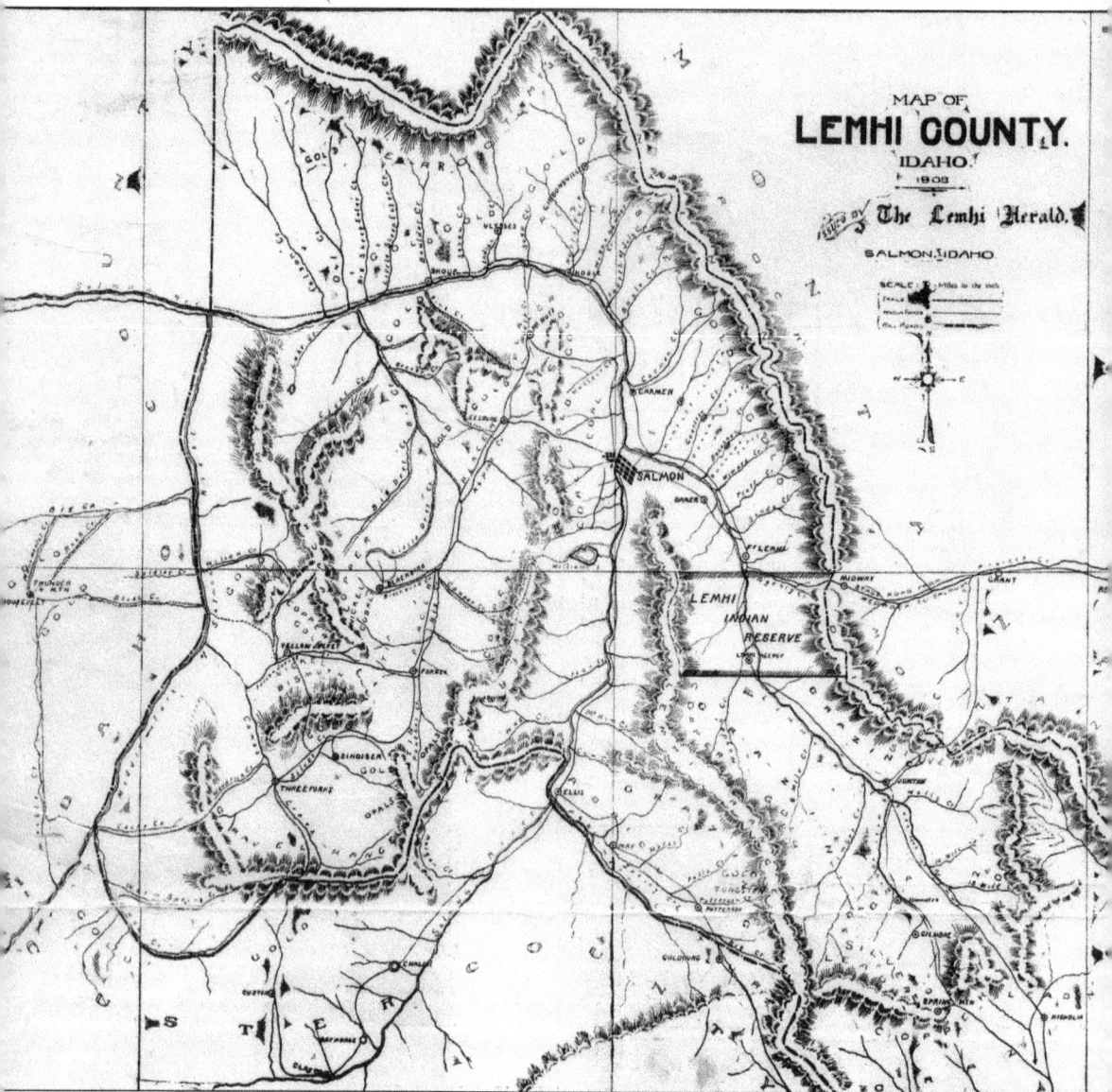

This map appeared in the April 23, 1908, issue of the Salmon City newspaper, *The Lemhi Herald*. Note the location of the Lemhi Reserve.

ON THE COVER: These early pioneers of Lemhi County gathered in the 1880s to have photographer W. B. Fowler take their picture in commemoration of their contributions to the area. They are standing in front of the Van Dreff cabin, built in 1866 by an enterprising man who remains, for the most part, a mystery. Even his first name is unknown. The first home built in Salmon City, it sat between North St. Charles and Terrace Streets and was torn down in 1905. Pictured here, from left to right, are A. J. McNab, W. J. Bryan, W. H. Andrew, Anthony Hornback, W. H. Shoup, M. M. McPherson, Peter Amonson, J. W. Davis, N. I. Andrews, W. C. Shoup, E. S. Edwards, and Jacob Finstur; (on the building) A. Barrack and George "Baldy" Martin, whose shoes are on the sidewalk in front. (Courtesy of the Lemhi County Historical Society and Museum.)

IMAGES
of America

LEMHI COUNTY

Hope Benedict and the Lemhi County
Historical Society and Museum

ARCADIA
PUBLISHING

Published by Arcadia Publishing
Charleston, South Carolina

Library of Congress Catalog Card Number: 2006920548

For all general information contact Arcadia Publishing at:
Telephone 843-853-2070
Fax 843-853-0044
E-mail sales@arcadiapublishing.com
For customer service and orders:
Toll-Free 1-888-313-2665

Visit us on the Internet at www.arcadiapublishing.com

*This book is dedicated to my parents, E. Richard and Bernice
Moore Benedict, and to the memory of William J. Cannon
(1917–1992)—my favorite back-roads traveling and storytelling
companions. It is also dedicated to my husband, Stewart
Carrington, who is always patient when I retell their stories and
sometimes interested but always my own captive audience.*

CONTENTS

ACKNOWLEDGMENTS

On behalf of the Lemhi County Historical Society and Museum, I would like to thank all those who have entrusted us with their photograph collections and given us the opportunity to share their memories. I would like, particularly, to thank Rose Corum, for it is her love of history and her devotion to the museum that have enabled the society to persevere. In fact, the entire crew of the museum deserves recognition for the hours they have committed to making our institution a great one: Rose Corum, Virginia Crismon, Audrey Nichols, Clair Wiley, Alberta Wiederrick, Cheryl and Lloyd Jones, Dolly Lewis, Gladys Smith, Gladys Swanson, Rose and Bill Bolton, Chuck Kane, Dale Ford, Dave Call, Luann Chandler, and Sue Dickens, as well as all members of the society.

Although all of our photographs are priceless, we have a number of collections that have been invaluable, and I would like to acknowledge those donations of the following in particular: the Kenneth and Doris Yearian family collection, the Pern family collection, the Don Pyeatt/Clyde Stone collection, the Don Mulkey collection, and the Herb St. Clair collection. A number of people also contributed photographs for this project from their private family collections, and I want to thank them—Rose and William Bolton, Clair and Jim Wiley, Rose Corum, the Seth Daniels family, Arden and Anne Westfall, Teddy Miller, Toots Perry, Dee Keirnes, Phil Shenon, Ralph and Gayle Nichols, E. Richard and Bernice Benedict, Mary Daniels, Steve and Norma Mahaffey, Patt Havens Asplund, Kay and Clyde Chaffin, Thelma Kesl, Jack McKinney, and Elaine Langfitt Wing and family—and thank you, too, to anyone I may have forgotten. In addition, I would like to thank the Salmon-Challis National Forest and the Idaho State Historical Society, Library, and Archives for the use of their photographs; Angie Hurley and Ann Marie Ojala of the Sacajawea Interpretive, Cultural, and Educational Center; and Antonio Hedrick of the Boise BLM office for their research. I would also like to thank John Benedict of Canada, who happened by at just the right time and gave me an invaluable lesson on haying equipment; Bambi Brown McAfee for helping in the selection process; and Louise Wagenknect for reading the text.

This project could not have been completed without those who helped me pore over our many photographs and who made me choose when I wanted to include them all. Special thanks must be reserved, however, for Rose and Bill Bolton, Clair Wiley, and Bernice and Richard Benedict, who spent countless hours not only helping with photographs, providing information, and reading text but reassuring me.

All photographs without a specific credit are part of the general collection of the Lemhi County Historical Society and Museum.

And as with any history project conducted in Lemhi County, a special debt is owed to the Lemhi County History Book Committee, whose *Centennial History of Lemhi County* has become the county's best reference.

INTRODUCTION

In June 1866, five prospectors—Frank Sharkey, Ward Girton, Elijah Mulkey, William Smith, and Joseph Rapp—armed with rumors of gold in the mountains surrounding the Lemhi Valley, left the gold fields of Montana and prospected their way to the present-day location of Salmon City, Idaho. Their test holes found no trace of ore, however, until mid-July. Crossing the river in a hand-hewn boat, the erstwhile miners struck gold in what is now the Salmon River Range near Napias (a Shoshone word for gold) Creek. Having fought the elements for several weeks, including snow, steep rocky mountains, and a river swollen from the spring runoff, the prospective millionaires determined to keep their find a secret until they could notify "just a few" of their friends. But the Lemhi Valley was not quite the isolated and undiscovered land for which they had hoped.

At the time of the gold strike, the Lemhi, Salmon, and Pahsimeroi Valleys were home to a people whose antecedents had been there at least 10,000 years. This region served as the traditional homeland for the Agaidika (salmon eaters), a Shoshonean tribe, now more commonly referred to as the Lemhi Shoshone. The Lemhis, the people of Sacajawea, had already gained national acclaim in 1806 with the successful return of the Lewis and Clark Corps of Discovery. In August 1805, assisted by Sacajawea, who had been kidnapped by the Hidatsas and then sold to the French-Canadian Toussaint Charbonneau, the weary and hungry crew finally located the Agaidika in the mountains of the Continental Divide. The corps' encounter with the Shoshone, along with their acquisition of horses and a temporary guide, Toby, mitigated, to a degree, the enormous difficulties of the ensuing weeks of winter-mountain travel and enabled them to complete their journey.

The demand for furs in the eastern United States and Europe brought another type of adventurer in the 1820s. Trappers, including those of the Northwest Company and Hudson's Bay, made use of the three rivers and their valleys in their search for beaver pelts. Although the temporary disappearance of the beaver had moved them out by 1840, their familiarity with the region helped establish the way for missionaries and potential settlers.

In 1855, with directions from Brigham Young to settle among the "buffalo-hunting Flathead, Bannack [sic], or Shoshone Indians," a group of Latter-day Saints missionaries established the Salmon River Mission. More popularly known as "Fort Limhi," named after a figure in the Book of Mormon, the site they chose was over 300 hundred miles from their Utah home, situated along the banks of the river near the camping site of Lewis and Clark, and near the favored camping area of the Agaidika in their homeland Agai Pah (the Lemhi Valley).

Although it would be impossible to calculate the long-term effect of their religious ministrations upon the indigenous population, they initially developed a cooperative relationship with the Shoshone, as well as with the Bannock and Nez Perce, who frequented the region during the salmon runs. But a number of insurmountable problems, including intertribal difficulties and a growing mistrust between the missionaries and the tribes, undermined their early successes and forced the dissolution of the mission. In March 1858, having lost three men during cattle raids against the fort, they deemed evacuation imperative.

Despite the brevity of their mission, Fort Limhi made a lasting imprint. The region became known as "Lemhi" and the name was eventually applied to the river beside which the fort was constructed, to the mountain range across the valley, to the mountain pass over which the Corps of Discovery traveled with Sacajawea, and, in 1869, to the county itself. The Agaidika, too, use the appellation "Lemhi" Shoshone to differentiate themselves from the "Fort Hall" Shoshone and to maintain regional identification.

The 1866 discovery of gold, then, was simply another incursion into the land of the Agaidika. But this time, it was not temporary. By August 1866, prospectors streamed into the area and continuous mineral discoveries in the region kept miners and community builders coming. Frank Sharkey, who had already staked significant claims and could afford to bide his time, set up a successful business ferrying new arrivals to the west bank of the river—he made $585 the first day at $2.50 per person per crossing. From there, prospectors embarked on the steep and often difficult trail to the placer fields and the thriving mountain community of Leesburg. As early as 1867, however, the encampment near the Salmon River, which had simply served as a launching pad, replaced Leesburg as the primary metropolis. More accessible than its mountain counterpart, Salmon City soon became the regional trade center for the developing mines and, in January 1869, the seat of county government.

Further discoveries of gold, lead-silver, copper, tungsten, cobalt, and other minerals, helped create a regional community that included not only small mining camps but substantial towns, specifically Shoup, Gibbonsville, Nicholia, Gilmore, and later, Cobalt. However, it was the simultaneous evolution of the ranching and timber industries that ensured a more stable economy and the consequent commitment to place.

But this same growth and economic expansion eventually displaced the indigenous population. Insecurity and a growing demand for land and water among the new settlers relegated the Agaidika to a reservation within their homeland as early as 1868. Their sense of place and the strong leadership of Chief Tendoy enabled them to withstand extreme pressure from the federal government, and often untenable conditions, until 1907, when they were forced to remove to Fort Hall. Agai Pah remains their traditional home, however, and the Bicentennial Commemoration of the Corps of Discovery and Sacajawea's role in the trek have helped the Lemhi Shoshone, the City of Salmon, and the Idaho Governor's Lewis and Clark Trail Committee establish the Sacajawea Interpretive, Cultural, and Educational Center along the banks of the Lemhi River.

With this photographic history of Lemhi County, the Lemhi County Historical Society recognizes a past that cannot help but shape our future.

One

THE AGAIDIKA

The traditional homeland of the Agaidika, or the Lemhi Shoshone, encompasses a large area, but most of the year they lived in the Lemhi, Salmon, and Pahsimeroi Valleys, moving throughout the region as necessary. Although relegated to a reservation in the Lemhi Valley after 1868, the relationship that Chief Tendoy and his people engendered with the new mining and ranching community allowed for some freedom of movement. This photograph was taken above Salmon City, near Jesse Creek, c. 1900.

Chief Tendoy became chief of the 500–700 Lemhi Shoshone in 1863 and continued to lead his people until his death on May 10, 1907. Becoming chief just three years before the Napias Creek gold rush, he had little time to prepare for what would become his most difficult role—ensuring the safety of his people. Within one year of the gold strike, five fishing weirs had been installed on the Lemhi River, precluding the movement of fish upstream to spawn and destroying a substantial portion of the Agaidika's food supply; their lands were being claimed by the ever-increasing number of miners and ranchers; and in 1868, they were placed on a provisional reservation and offered a treaty. Although Tendoy and his people agreed to the conditions, the treaty was never ratified. Negotiations continued, thanks primarily to the efforts of Chief Tendoy, but as they dragged on, conditions for the Lemhis deteriorated. It was not until 1875 that a more permanent arrangement was made and a reservation was established through an executive order issued by Pres. U. S. Grant on February 12 of that year.

This is Chief Tendoy's third wife, Ta Gwah Wee, with whom Tendoy had seven children, one of whom died in infancy. Tendoy had three wives and 16 children, but several died young and four died in infancy. The deaths were attributed primarily to the poor conditions on the reservation. The dress overlay she is wearing was made of elk teeth.

This photograph of a Lemhi family was taken near Jesse Creek above Salmon City, *c.* 1900.

This photograph of Lemhi Shoshone teepees was taken near Salmon City, *c.* 1900. (Courtesy of the Bolton family.)

Pictured here are Tooe-Pompe (also spelled Toopompey), son of Chief Tendoy, and Jack Grouse, right. Tooe-Pompe was the father of 12 children, seven of whom died in infancy.

This photograph was taken during a Lemhi Indian council held on the Island Park, c. 1900. Pictured here, from left to right, are (first row) Poorman (identified on the Lemhi County Historical Museum's photograph as Chief Tendoy's son), John Tyler, Johnson Keni-botts, Frank Wahtomy, and Jack Grouse (also identified as Queena Moby or "Chicken Nose"); (second row) William Burton and Benjamin Tyone.

This 1922 photograph of Archie Nappo (also spelled Napo) was taken by Don Pyeatt, a rancher and photographer in the Lemhi Valley. Nappo, according to Pyeatt's records, came to him and asked for the photograph to be taken. Pyeatt's photograph collection includes a number of images from the reservation (which closed in 1907) and other scenes from early Lemhi County.

This photograph was taken from a *c.* 1920 postcard. Across the top, the producer of the card printed, "Two Lemhi Shoshone women." They are holding between them what appears to be a feathered headdress. Traditionally, after the 17th century, clothing was made from elk skin and decorated with quillwork or beads. Women wore dresses with knee-length leggings and frequently wore elk-tooth necklaces.

The Lemhi Indian Agency, established by executive order in 1875, comprised approximately 100 square miles and "same hereby is, withdrawn from sale and set apart for the exclusive use of the mixed tribes of Shoshone, Bannock, and Sheepeater Indians, to be known as the Lemhi Valley Indian Reservation." The building in this photograph is the boardinghouse for agency employees; note that the flag is flying upside—a sign of distress. In the front row are unidentified members of the Lemhi Shoshones. The agency employees, from left to right, are (second row, porch) Mrs. DeSylum, cook; unidentified; J. M. Needham, Indian agent; Belle Rees, teacher and cook; and Dr. W. C. Whitwell, agency doctor; (third row, balcony) Mr. Porter, teacher; Porter's child; Mrs. Porter; Will Kadletz, blacksmith; Bob Stocker, boss farmer; and Ben Tyler, cook.

The agency police, who were members of the Lemhi Shoshone tribe, are pictured here around 1890.

Pictured here around 1900 are the children of the Agaidika. Assimilation was the primary goal of the federal government's 19th-century policy toward the Native Americans. It's twin objectives were to inculcate Caucasian belief systems, dress, agrarianism, and language while destroying any trace of the Native American culture.

Discipline was strict on the reservation and schoolchildren were marched from class to class.

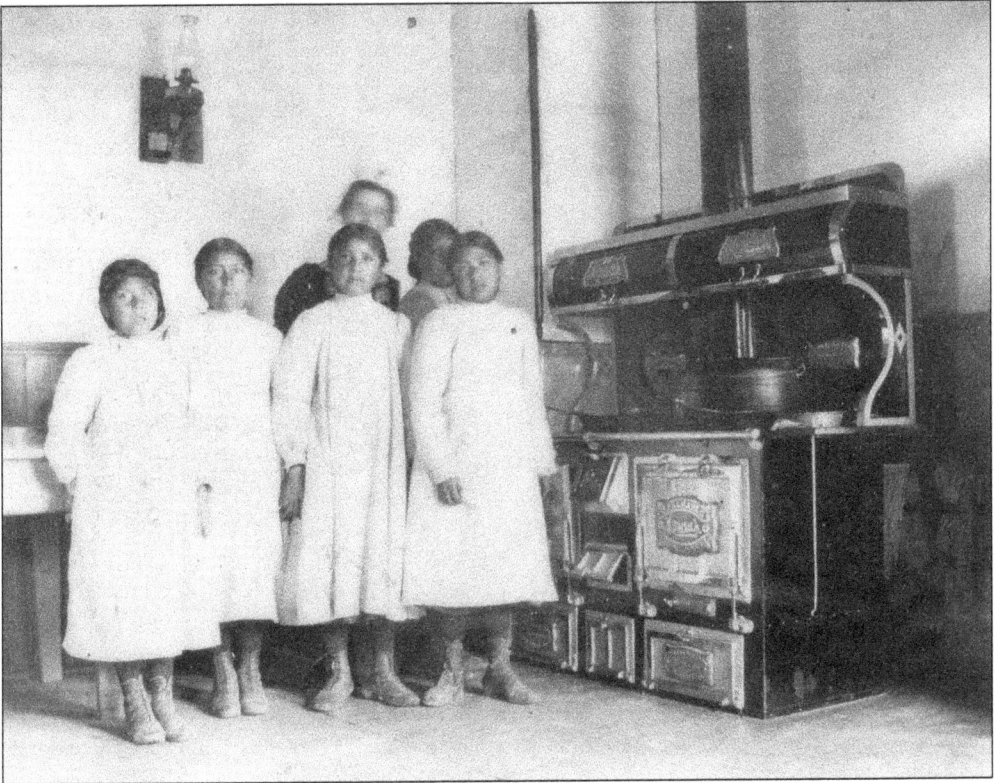

As is evidenced by these two photographs, an important part of the assimilation process for girls was in the "art of home-economics."

Pictured in these two photographs are school groups of Agaidika boys. The larger, younger class below is pictured with their teacher, identified as either Helen or Adele Sharkey (both children of Frank Sharkey).

Pictured, from left to right, are M. M. McPherson, Chief Tendoy, and Jack Tendoy, the chief's son. Tendoy considered McPherson and George L. Shoup friends, and they did, occasionally, interceded on Tendoy's behalf wit the Indian agents and the Idaho Territorial (prior to 1890) delegate to Washington, D.C., John Hailey.

Tendoy's young son, Chief Tendoy, and an unidentified man were photographed near Leesburg, Idaho, the earliest mining town in Lemhi County, c. 1890. (Courtesy of the Pern family.)

This photograph appears to have been taken on a holiday. Note the band standing behind the fence. Although no member of the Lemhi Shoshone is identified, a number of agency employees are listed as being present and are as follows: John Rees, Billy Kadletz, ? Bresher, Jim Dysert, Don Pyeatt, John Pugh, E. M. Yearian, and Leo Pyeatt. E. M Yearian was one of the agents, serving from 1897 to 1904.

Chief Tendoy,
Salmon, Idaho.

Chief Tendoy continued working for the welfare of his people throughout his life. Invited in 1880 to Washington, D.C., along with three other Lemhis and representatives from the Fort Hall Reservation, an agreement was reached by which the Lemhis would remove to Fort Hall to lands ceded to them by the Fort Hall tribal government. Each group would receive payment—the Lemhis for their reservation in the Lemhi Valley and the Fort Hall tribe for their cession of lands for Lemhi occupation. When Tendoy returned to the Lemhi Reservation, the Lemhis refused to leave their home and Tendoy informed local leader, George Shoup, who in turn informed the federal officials that the Lemhis would not be leaving. The treaty was not ratified, in fact, until 1889, when a final section stipulated that the Lemhis would not be removed to Fort Hall until a majority of the adult males agreed to do so. That did not happen until the end of December 1905. The decision was accepted in 1906, and the Lemhis moved in the early summer of 1907, shortly after the death of their chief.

Two

FORT LIMHI

JOHN E. REES, R.B.HERNDON, JUDGE SHURTLIFF

The Church of Jesus Christ of Latter-day Saints established the Salmon River Mission, or "Fort Limhi," in 1855, but circumstances forced them to abandon it in 1858. Pictured here during a 1914 commemoration, from left to right, are John E. Rees, R. B. Herndon, and Judge L. W. Shurtliff, who was one of the original Salmon River missionaries. (Courtesy of the Idaho State Historical Society.)

Within two years, the missionaries had built a mud fort, constructed cabins, dug a community well, developed the first irrigation system in Idaho, and attracted more than 100 settlers. R. B. Herndon, left, is shown shaking hands with John E. Rees over Lemhi County's first irrigation ditch.

After visiting the fort in May 1857 with 142 companions, Young enthusiastically proclaimed the success of their mission, but the next 10 months proved his proclamation premature. In March 1858, the missionary community returned to Utah. This photograph shows the parameters of the mud wall and a couple of cabins in the background. Today the wall has all but disappeared. (Courtesy of the Idaho State Historical Society.)

Three

MINING
FROM GOLD TO COBALT

From the 1866 discovery of gold, mining played a key role in the economic development of Lemhi County. This picture demonstrates the use of a sluice box through which miners channeled gravel and water. The wood slats on the bottom of the trough created riffles in the water, causing the heavier gold particles to catch against the slats and the lighter dirt and gravel to wash through. (Courtesy of the Pern family.)

This photograph, taken near Leesburg, depicts hydraulic mining and the use of a "giant." In this process, water is brought around a hillside from above and then channeled into a pipe which gets progressively smaller, thereby increasing the pressure. The water is forced through a cast iron nozzle (the giant) and used to "wash" the gravel away from the mountainside. The gravel is then channeled through a large version of the sluice box. (Courtesy of the Pern family.)

This dredge on Moose Creek offers another example of hydraulic mining. Gravel is scraped from underneath, brought into the dredge on conveyors, and then, with a system much like the sluice box, is separated from the ore. The residue is then deposited behind, creating large piles as it goes. The use of water for the washing and separating processes essentially creates a lake in which this boat-like apparatus functions.

This photograph of the gold dredge on Kirtley Creek clearly shows the lake and the piles of gravel created by the dredging process. Smaller placer operations started on Kirtley Creek in 1890; dredging began after 1910.

This photograph of the tunnel and mine car of the Gold Ridge Mining Company came from the O. E. Kirkpatrick collection, housed at the Lemhi County Museum. Kirkpatrick, one of the area's most distinctive characters, mined the "Gold Dust Group" in the Leesburg area, beginning operations in 1896. When his days as a miner drew to a close, he remained in Leesburg to write the town's history and to commemorate the memories of those first mining pioneers.

Once the surface placers were mined, lode mining, or underground mining, began in earnest. Tunnels were dug, timbers were placed along the walls and the ceiling to prevent cave-ins, and ore cars brought the gravel out for the separation of the ore from the waste. (Courtesy of the Pern family.)

This photograph depicts the mill at the Pope-Shenon Mine, located on Sal Mountain eight miles south of Salmon City. A copper mine, the Pope-Shenon lode was initially developed by two of the county's early pioneers, miner and rancher Thomas Pope and businessman and rancher Phil Shenon; it was operated intermittently into the mid-20th century. (Courtesy of Rose Corum.)

The Harmony Mine (the mill is seen above) was another of the area's copper mines and was located at the head of Withington Creek. A substantial operation, it was first developed in 1916 and was rumored to have been owned, for a time, by members of the mafia. (Courtesy of Rose Corum.)

This photograph displays the internal operations of a stamp mill. Stamps, or heavy weights, are raised mechanically and then dropped to break the gravel down even further. Although not specifically identified, it is probably O. E. Kirkpatrick's Gold Dust Stamp Mill or the mill for the Italian Mine, both of which were located in the Mackinaw District near Leesburg.

This is the head frame for the new shaft at the AD&M Mine (American Development, Mining, and Reduction Company) in Gibbonsville, Idaho, in 1890. Operating through the 1890s, the AD&M Company erected a 30-stamp mill with cyanide and chlorination plants. When it ceased operation in 1899, the company mines had produced $1.5 million in gold. (Courtesy of the Salmon-Challis National Forest.)

"Queen of the Hills" Mine, near Salmon, Idaho.

In the early 1880s, the Queen of the Hills Mine was located on Derier Gulch but remained undeveloped until the Copper Queen Mining Company initiated operations in 1898. (Courtesy of Rose Corum.)

To facilitate ore production at the Viola Mine, 16 kilns were constructed above Birch Creek in the Nicholia Mining District. They burned approximately 2 million board feet of timber to produce the charcoal necessary for the smelter at the Viola lead-silver mine. The mine, which operated from 1882 to 1889, and the Viola mining engineer, Ralph Nichols, also helped stimulate an interest in the Texas District Mines, of which Nichols's mine, the Latest Out, was one of the largest producers in the first decades of the 20th century.

This photograph of the Ima Mine, near Patterson in the Pahsimeroi Valley, depicts the tramline bringing ore to the mill from the tunnels. To the right is the waterline. Discovered in 1881, mining began in earnest under the direction of the Ima Consolidated Mining and Milling Company in 1900. The tungsten deposits for which it became important were not recognized until 1903 and not the primary focus until 1911. (Courtesy of Teddy Miller.)

The Blackbird Mine produced over $47 million worth of cobalt, copper, and gold during its long history. Although mined intermittently from the 1880s, its most productive period occurred in the 20th century due to the increased demand for cobalt alloys during World War I and World War II. A short-lived mining venture during World War I convinced local mining men, including Jim Sims, the Howe-Sound Company of New York, and Gibbons and Reed of Salt Lake City, of the feasibility and necessity of producing cobalt in this remote region during the 1940s. Tunnels were excavated and at war's end, the Blackbird Mine reopened under the Calera Mining Company. The heaviest production came between 1951 and 1959. The company town of Cobalt, which was built seven miles from the mines, included a school, grocery store, recreation hall, and individual homes and apartments. It had a population over 1,500. The mill, right, housed both ball and rod mills. One can also see the tramline and, to the far left, the main, or lower, tunnel. (Courtesy of the Salmon-Challis National Forest.)

This is the underground lunchroom at the Blackbird Mine in the main or lower tunnel, also known as the "6850" because of its elevation of 6,850 feet. Note the miner standing in the tunnel. (Courtesy of the Salmon-Challis National Forest.)

During the latter half of the 1950s, an open pit was dug at the Blackbird Mine to facilitate ore production. The mine ceased operations in 1960 but experienced another five years of production between 1965 and 1970. The Blackbird Mine contributed significantly to the economic stability of Lemhi County during the mid-20th century. (Courtesy of E. Richard Benedict.)

Gibbonsville gold miners are pictured here in 1880 with their sluice box. Pictured, from left to right, are Charlie Lual and the Wonderlick Boys. Prospectors discovered gold in the Gibbonsville District in 1877 along Anderson Creek, and mining continued there well into the 20th century. Although the AD&M Company controlled most of the producing mining claims during the 1890s, other groups with patented claims produced substantial gold, including the Clara Morris Group, which had produced about $250,000 by 1908 and the Twin Brothers Group, which had produced approximately $300,000 by that same year.

In 1895, the Ulysses Mine was located on Indian Creek down the Salmon River, but it was not developed until 1901, when the Kittie Burton Mining Company purchased the two main-lode deposits in the district—the Kittie Burton and the Ulysses. The company opened operations in 1902. The primary reason for delay was transportation problems. Although the scows, bound for the mines near Shoup, floated directly by Indian Creek, transporting supplies and equipment from the Salmon River to the mines above was an arduous task. Pictured here are the miners at the Ulysses boardinghouse. From left to right, they are Doug Buster, William Mahaffey, Thomas Boyle, Harry Cannon, Gregor Anderson, William ?, William Warner, ? Hewitson, Ed McMann, Ola Smout, Win Smout, unidentified, F. Cowell, Fred Rose, unidentified, Dan Kane, Theo Ketchum, and Joe Vaughn.

Pictured here are the miners and the mill at Meyers Cove, c. 1900. Prospectors discovered gold and silver there as early as 1875, but little serious development occurred before 1896. This mill may be the production center for the Monument Mine. (Courtesy of O. E. Kirkpatrick.)

These miners are in a tunnel near Shoup. Neither the miners nor the mine are identified, but gold mining was widespread down the Salmon River. Independent prospectors operated placer mines as early as 1868, but lode mining developed later and lasted into the early 20th century.

Miners are setting up mining equipment in a Lemhi County mine. Although the location of the mine remains a mystery, it may be the Ranger Mine on Geertson Creek. (Courtesy of the Bolton family.)

This photograph depicts the miners at one of the mines in the Texas District near Gilmore. Note their hard hats with the carbide lamps for underground work. Prospectors discovered the rich lead-silver mines in the region as early as the 1880s, but problems with the market and transportation delayed serious development until 1910.

Dated 1880, this is one of the earliest photographs available of Leesburg. (Courtesy of the Pern family.)

In this photograph of the Yellow Jacket Mine, the most visible element is the Yellow Jacket Hotel, which was built in the early 1900s as a promotional venture. Primarily, however, it served the miners who worked at the gold mine. Discovered in 1868, the mine was operated intermittently during the 20th century, primarily by the Steen family.

This was the Gibbonsville Post Office around 1910. (Courtesy of Herb St. Clair.)

According to available information, this Gibbonsville grocery store, pictured here in 1910, was opened by the AD&M Company. Offering foodstuffs on this side, the other side was devoted to clothing.

This 1890 photograph of Gibbonsville was developed from a glass slide. Its clarity enables the viewer to understand how over 2,000 people once lived in the narrow canyons of Dahlonega and Anderson Creeks. (Courtesy of the Wiley family.)

This photograph of the community of Shoup and the Shoup pack bridge was taken in 1909 by the railroad survey crew. Mining down the Salmon River began as early as 1868 and continued well into the 20th century. (Courtesy of the Seth Daniels family.)

This photograph of Nicholia's Main Street was taken in the mid-1880s. Named after the mining engineer and mine director, Ralph Nichols, Nicholia served as the community for the Viola Mine. The town offered a boardinghouse and community organizations, as well as lead poisoning from the smelter operations.

The town of Gilmore evolved during the development of lead-silver, or galena, mines in the Texas District. Although the minerals were discovered as early as the 1880s, mining was delayed until 1902 because of market issues and the trials of transporting ore over long distances. Initially it was just a camp next to the mines. When Pennsylvania mining money brought a railroad to the region, the town moved to a lower clime—7,200 feet. With restaurants, saloons, pool halls, a theater, a meat market, hospital, company houses, boardinghouses, and individual homes, Gilmore grew to a community of over 600 during the 1910s and early 1920s. (Courtesy of the Bolton family.)

Pictured here is the Benedict and Wentworth Meat Market of Gilmore. It was opened in 1909 by John Benedict and Lee Wentworth to accommodate the construction workers of the Gilmore and Pittsburgh Railroad. It was eventually owned and operated by Thomas and Ruby Benedict. Pictured here, from left to right, are Thomas Benedict, Bill Tweedy Jr. (in the car), Al Ziems, Bill Tweedy Sr., and Floyd Owens. (Courtesy of E. Richard Benedict.)

The Gilmore Mercantile, pictured here c. 1915, served as the post office and supply center for the community of Gilmore and was operated by Grover and Elmer Tucker, members of the Pennsylvania entourage who facilitated mining operations and transportation in the Texas District.

The Leadville lead-silver mine, located just outside the town of Junction, operated during the first decades of the 20th century. Pictured here are investors and mining camp residents; in the background, the mill and tailings are visible.

Although many Lemhi County mines generated mining camps and towns, many miners operated on their own. Pictured here are two miners at the Joseph and Geoff Hot Springs Mine on Owl Creek. (Courtesy of Herb St. Clair.)

Four

RANCHING
FROM RAISING HAY TO
RIDING MUSTANGS

Clyde Starr stands astride a team of horses in the midst of a herd of cattle at feeding time on the Barrack Ranch, where he was the foreman. Starr, who married Cassie McKinney, later owned and operated the Geertson Creek Ranch. Their daughter Rose Starr Bolton and her husband, William Bolton, along with their daughter Merry and her husband, David Logan, operated the Geertson ranch into the 21st century. (Courtesy of the Bolton family.)

Pictured here around 1890 is the Shenon Ranch, established by Phil Shenon as part of his Shenon Land and Livestock Company. The ranch was later owned by, among others, Chris Nielson, Emmett and Eleanor Steele Reese, and the Stephenson family. It has long been one of the finest ranches in Lemhi County. (Courtesy of the Bolton family.)

Frank Sharkey established this ranch near Tendoy after several years of successful mining in the Leesburg Basin. Unlike many 19th-century miners who simply tramped from strike to strike, Sharkey, along with a number of his compatriots, considered Lemhi County his home. The ranch was later owned by the Mahaffey family and is now known as the Muleshoe Ranch. Fort Limhi is located on this property. (Courtesy of the Steve Mahaffey family.)

Sheep comprised an important part of the agricultural market during the late 19th and early 20th centuries. Most ranchers, in addition to their cattle, raised sheep. Albert Smith (grandfather of Clair Wiley) herded these sheep for the Mahaffeys. This photograph was probably taken near Forney. (Courtesy of the Wiley family.)

Pictured here is the sheep-shearing process on the Stone Ranch near Leadore, Idaho. (Courtesy of Rose Corum.)

Peter McKinney, who arrived in Lemhi County in 1890, was an entrepreneur with a keen business sense. Beginning as a cook at the Gibbonsville mines, he later moved into ranching, retail, and mining. His Lemhi Irrigation and Orchard Company operated a number of ranches in Lemhi and Custer Counties and included this sheep-shearing station on the Salmon River. (Courtesy of the Bolton family.)

Most ranches raised hogs, and the Geertson Creek Ranch was no different. (Courtesy of the Bolton family.)

Lemhi County is not usually considered part of the "potato country" of Idaho; however, potatoes were an important crop for early ranchers as well as for many 20th-century area farmers, including the Stokes family, who operated a large potato farm just outside of Salmon City. This photograph was taken on the Geertson Creek Ranch as potatoes were being hauled to market. (Courtesy of the Bolton family.)

Every farming and ranching family also had dairy cows, or at least one or two milk cows. Clair (Bolander) Wiley, the daughter of Red and Irene Smith Bolander, poses here with the family milk cow in the Pahsimeroi Valley. Irene Bolander taught in the valley, and Red Bolander operated a ranch there in the late 1930s. (Courtesy of the Wiley family.)

Hay production has always been an important part of the ranching industry in Lemhi County, as demonstrated by this early haying process in the Lemhi Valley using a Jackson fork derrick. (Courtesy of Clyde Stone and Don Pyeatt.)

In this photograph, haying is done with the use of the overshot derrick on the Ernest Benedict ranch (now the Carl Ellsworth ranch) near Leadore. (Courtesy of E. Richard Benedict.)

Here hay is being transferred from windrows onto a hay wagon. Picked up with a sweep, it is then transferred through the chute to the wagon, which will take the hay to the stack. (Courtesy of the Bolton and Withington families.)

Ranchers also produced grain. In this photograph, a horse-drawn binder is shocking the grain. After drying, it was loaded on a wagon and then run through the threshing machine. (Courtesy of Clyde Stone and Don Pyeatt.)

The wide valley of the Pahsimeroi helped create a number of large ranches. Here an early threshing machine threshes the grain. A horse-powered drive shaft is running from the horses in the background to the thresher on the wagon in the foreground. Looking closely, one can see a man with a whip standing in the middle of the horses driving them around the turnstile, which is creating the power.

A young Clyde Starr, who, with his wife, Cassie McKinney Starr, owned and operated a ranch on Geertson Creek, poses as a "gun-slinging" cowboy of western lore, c. 1910. (Courtesy of the Bolton family.)

This young cowboy is Frank Schwartz of the Pahsimeroi and Lemhi Valleys. He was killed serving in World War I. (Courtesy of the Marsing family.)

Bronco Henry Williams, the regionally famous cowboy, takes a break from a 1915 rodeo. It is said that he once roped and rode a mountain goat, and that he beat a worthy challenger in a bronc-riding contest by riding his horse backwards in a rear-facing saddle. It is for him that Williams Lake, Williams Creek, and Henry Creek are named. (Courtesy of the Ralph and Gayle Nichols family of Belgrade, Montana.)

Lemhi County has had a long tradition of late-summer rodeos. Many of the earliest took place on ranches, including the George Barrows ranch above Leadore, the Haynes Creek Ranch of Charlie Snook, the Long Ranch north of town, and in the Pahsimeroi Valley. Note that one cowboy is bracing himself against a horse and biting the ear of the bronc being saddled. (Courtesy of the Ralph and Gayle Nichols family.)

Early ranchers in the county periodically rounded up one of the herds of mustangs that roamed the foothills, selected the most likely candidates, and set about the "training" process. This usually initiated an impromptu rodeo. Rather than having his ear bitten, this horse has been blindfolded against the task at hand. (Courtesy of the Bolton family.)

This rodeo took place on Carmen Creek around 1910. (Courtesy of the Bolton family.)

Local ranchers and cowboys used the rodeos and roundups to demonstrate their prowess at western living. (Courtesy of the Ralph and Gayle Nichols family.)

No place was off limits for a demonstration of skill. This photograph was taken in front of the old Carmen Post Office. (Courtesy of the Bolton family.)

This photograph was taken on the Isley Ranch on the Big Flat. (Courtesy of the Wiley family.)

In 1925, Charlie Walchli stands with "Headlight" and a saddle horse on C. A. Norton's shorthorn cattle ranch in the Salmon Valley on the Big Flat. (Courtesy of the Wiley family.)

All one can see of this cowboy are his woolly chaps and cowboy boots as he stands on his head in the saddle, showing off for his companions. Although ranch work was difficult, there was often time for fun. (Courtesy of the Bolton family.)

Joe Mulkey sits astride his horse on the Gus Mulkey ranch on Lee Creek near Leadore. (Courtesy of Don Mulkey.)

Five

THE TIMBER INDUSTRY

The timber industry was an important third component of the 19th- and 20th-century local economy. Within a few years of the first placer mining, portable, individually owned sawmills dotted the mountainsides. Early logging was often done with horses. Trees were cut down and horses brought the load to the mill, as shown in this photograph taken near the Panther Creek Sawmill owned by Frank and Mary Daniels. (Courtesy of Mary Daniels.)

The timber industry provided wood not only for building homes and businesses but also for the developing lode-mining industry. Underground mining required timber for framing the tunnel against possible cave-ins. This photograph was taken near Leesburg, c. 1900. (Courtesy of the Pern family.)

Several teams of horses pull an enormous wagon load of logs in Lemhi County, *c.* 1890. (Courtesy of Dee Keirnes.)

Before chain saws, cutting timber was often a two-man job, demonstrated in this photograph of two men operating a crosscut saw. (Courtesy of the Salmon-Challis National Forest.)

Large mining operations often had their own sawmills to produce the timber needed for mining. Pictured here is the Blackbird Mine's sawmill, *c.* 1955. Managed by Arden Westfall, the sawmill provided a number of jobs to local men, including Jerry Westfall (Arden's brother), Earl Perry and his son Charles, Eddie Fields, and Ed Hayes. (Courtesy of the Salmon-Challis National Forest.)

Sawmills throughout the county produced as much as 2 million board feet per year. During World War II, individual mill production reached as much as 5 million. Larger sawmills, like this one on Panther Creek, owned and operated by Frank and Mary Daniels, produced lumber for markets in Idaho and Montana, as well as outside the Intermountain West. (Courtesy of Mary Daniels.)

This Idaho Forest Products truck is parked in the yard of the sawmill and burner in Salmon City. Operated last as Salmon Intermountain Lumber, it was located where Saveway now stands. (Courtesy of the Salmon-Challis National Forest.)

The Westfall family has long been a prominent name in the local timber industry. This photograph of their logging truck was taken near Cobalt. (Courtesy of Arden and Anne Westfall.)

The Daniels operated their mill, which had originally been owned by Max Oyler, from 1937 to its sale in 1962. Taken around 1945, this photograph demonstrates just how difficult transporting logs can be. (Courtesy of Mary Daniels.)

Six

THE TRIALS
OF TRANSPORTATION

Transporting people, goods, and services into, out of, and throughout Lemhi County has never been an easy task. This photograph, taken about 1875, shows a row of packs across Salmon City's Main Street with goods bound for the mines. In the background stands the original pack bridge over the Salmon River, and on the far right, a business is advertised as the Miners' Brewery and Bakery.

Getting the pack string ready was a frequent scene on the streets of the county's primary trading center, Salmon City. This photograph was taken around 1890 on Center Street. (Courtesy of Myra Laurence.)

In the early 20th century, a pack string is taking goods down the Salmon River. It may have been loaded with supplies for the 1909 Salmon River survey, which was undertaken to determine the feasibility of a railroad track down the Salmon River canyon.

The stages pictured here are heavily loaded and stopped in front of the Shenon block, just east of the Shenon house itself. In the background, on the left, the original Methodist church is visible.

The freight wagon pictured here on Cottom Lane in 1909 was operated by Laurence Lipe and Bert Ellis. Some teams of horses were known as "jerkline" teams because the lead horses were trained to respond to a certain number of jerks on a single rope, rather than responding to reins.

Around 1900, Charlie Beach, renowned driver for the Redrock and Salmon River Stageline, is pictured here on Lemhi Pass (once known as the Agency Creek Pass). These stages, sometimes incorrectly labeled Concords, were actually "mud wagons" and were much lighter for easier travel on steep mountain roads. The "White Six," as Charlie's horses were known, could readily pull the mud wagon up the steep grade to the pass. The Redrock and Salmon River Stageline operated from 1886 to 1910, when the Gilmore and Pittsburgh Railroad made its operation unnecessary. On the trip from Redrock, Montana, to Salmon City, the stage stopped at Midway Station on the Montana side to change teams. The route followed by the stage was along the Shoshone trail that Lewis and Clark had traveled in 1805 into Lemhi County.

Peter McKinney stands beside the stage parked on Andrews Street next to the Shenon House, c. 1897. (Courtesy of the Bolton family.)

In this 1910 photograph, taken in front of George Shoup's Pioneer Mercantile, now the Ponderosa Gallery, the last Redrock and Salmon River Stageline leaves Salmon City. (Courtesy of the Shenon and Bolton families.)

With the coming of the Gilmore and Pittsburgh Railroad, stage travel ended in Lemhi County. In this 1910 photograph, the last stage from Junction to Gilmore prepares to leave.

Stage travel was not always the safest means of transportation, as evident in this c. 1900 photograph, probably taken near Lemhi Pass. (Courtesy of Dee Keirnes.)

Inclement weather made for ingenious transport of goods. In this c. 1910 photograph, a dogsled takes the mail to Forney. (Courtesy of Herb St. Clair.)

George and Dave Sandilands took goods and people via scows down the Salmon River to mines in the Shoup area. They reportedly took Capt. Harry Guleke on his first trip. After George drowned in the Pine Creek rapids, Dave searched the river for weeks for the body. Unsuccessful and heartbroken, he gave up his profession as river runner. Pictured in 1880, from left to right, are brothers Jim, George, and Dave. (Courtesy of E. Richard Benedict.)

Captain Guleke, the most famous of the local river runners, built his own scows at this boat-building yard just south of the Salmon River Bridge. The scows, constructed in town, were then "deconstructed" down the river and used for building materials.

On October 22, 1919, Captain Guleke, standing in the middle of the scow, and his crew set off for Riggins.

Loaded with supplies, scows embark from Salmon City on their downriver journey, c. 1900. (Courtesy of the Bolton family.)

The lure of the Salmon River and a Sunday boat ride are not recent developments, as evidenced by this c. 1915 photograph. (Courtesy of the Bolton family.)

A 1909 survey of the Salmon River Canyon convinced railroad enthusiasts and prospective investors that a rail line through the steep and rocky canyon was not feasible. Seth Daniels, pictured here, had a degree in engineering from Swarthmore College and proved indispensable to the project. (Courtesy of the Daniels family.)

The crew worked for six months, surveying and photographing the canyon. Their boats were 23 to 35 feet long, 13 to 14 feet wide, and equipped with all the necessities. (Courtesy of the Daniels family.)

Although equipped with all the necessities, once a month, a man brought in supplies by pack string, and these hunters were hired to provide fresh meat for the hardworking survey crew.

From 1866 to 1875, a toll bridge for foot traffic and pack animals spanned the Salmon River in downtown Salmon City; it was replaced in 1875 by a wooden structure. By 1905, it was deemed unsafe and replaced with this one. The sign on the bridge reads, "$5.00 fine for riding or driving over this bridge faster than a walk."

In 1926, this "Beauty Bridge" replaced the steel suspension bridge. And, although it has undergone modifications, it still serves as the connection between the east and west sides of town and safely transfers the traffic of Highway 93 from one side to the other. (Courtesy of the Benedict family.)

The railroad brought many changes to Lemhi County, and one of them was the eventual disappearance of the community of Junction. That city, located near the town of Leadore, reportedly refused to give the Gilmore and Pittsburgh Railroad Company land on which to build a station. So the railroad built its own town (Leadore) right next to it in 1910, and the business and social centers relocated.

Lead-silver provided the final impetus for a railroad. The transport of ore out of the county had always proved difficult, but the great amount of ore produced in the Gilmore mines proved more than the typical freighters could bear. This ingenious contraption, the steam-traction engine, had four ore cars and was introduced to help alleviate the costs of freighting ore 85 miles by freight wagon. It wore out after 12 trips in 1906. (Courtesy of Rose Corum.)

Pictured here around 1912 is the new Leadore Railroad Depot. (Courtesy of Luann Chandler.)

As early as the 1870s, county residents had longed for, demanded, and pleaded with railroad companies to bring their iron horses to East Central Idaho. Despite their assurances that Lemhi County, and especially Salmon City, would become the next Chicago, it was not until 1909 that the rich deposits of lead-silver in the Gilmore area made it a reality. It took just one year to build 118 miles of track over the 7,672-foot Bannock Pass from Armstead, Montana. The Gilmore and Pittsburgh train descended through the newly named Railroad Canyon on the Idaho side and arrived at the new depot in the new town of Leadore. There the line split, with one branch into Gilmore and the main line following the Lemhi River into Salmon City. A Golden Spike Ceremony on May 18, 1910, celebrated its completion. The G&P is pictured here with just one ore car loaded and headed up the canyon for Armstead.

Although the railroad was brought in with mining in mind, the entire community benefited from the new transportation, including the sheep growers, who shipped both wool and sheep on the train. (Courtesy of Rose Corum.)

This picture clearly shows just how much ore could be hauled out of Lemhi County for refining in the East. (Courtesy of Rose Corum.)

Unfortunately, however, the G&P suffered a number of finally insurmountable problems—among them, derailments.

And if derailments were not bad enough, there were always mountain slides, like this one on the Desmond Cut in 1920.

When the Lemhi River flooded, it was simply another in a series of disasters that precluded the Gilmore and Pittsburgh from being a long-term success. In fact, the G&P never made a profit and the company often had to forego repairs. By the 1920s, the Gilmore and Pittsburgh was more commonly known as the "Grunt and Pain" and the "Get out and Push."

This Brill railbus, affectionately known as the "Galloping Goose," worked in conjunction with the train and was often more efficient. It carried mail and passengers from Salmon to Leadore on Mondays, Wednesdays, and Fridays and from Salmon to Gilmore on Tuesdays, Thursdays, and Saturdays.

The introduction of truck lines did nothing to help the train, either. This wagon, affectionately known by its drivers as the "Good Ship Lollipop," carried goods, passengers, and eventually mail back and forth from Salmon, Challis, and Mackay. (Courtesy of the Benedict family.)

In the 1930s, with more trucks, and bigger ones, and an extensive highway system, the train did not stand a chance. The Benedict Truck Line, in addition to others, including Miller Brothers, could offer better rates and more reliable shipping. (Courtesy of the Benedict family.)

The proliferation of passenger cars, like this one parked in the middle of Salmon City's Main Street, also undermined the G&P. In 1939, the Gilmore and Pittsburgh Company president announced, "Effective May 1939, the Gilmore and Pittsburgh Railroad Company will discontinue operations of the railroad between Armstead, Montana[,] and Salmon, Idaho[,] because on that date the company will be without funds to continue operations." In 1940, the G&P made one last trip into Lemhi County. Then it backed out—from Salmon to Gilmore, back to Leadore, up Railroad Canyon, over the switchbacks, and to Armstead. As it went, the crews dismantled the rails and loaded them onto the train.

Seven

THE COMMUNITY OF LEMHI COUNTY

This picture of the "Founding Fathers" of Lemhi County was probably taken in 1910 during the railroad celebration. Pictured, from left to right, are (first row) James Kirtley, James Beattie, Charles Horton, and N. I. Andrews; (second row) M. M. McPherson, Thomas Pope, E. S. Edwards, James Hockensmith, and Eli Minert.

Frank Sharkey (1838–1919) was one of Lemhi County's earliest pioneers. One of the original five to discover gold in the Leesburg Basin, he owned and operated the Sharkey Ranch (now the Muleshoe Ranch) near Tendoy, and many of his descendants still live in the area. (Courtesy of the Langfitt family.)

By 1867, George Laird Shoup (1836–1904) was already contributing to the planning and development process of Salmon City. His first log store was built on Main Street in 1867. In 1886, his financial successes enabled the construction of a three-story mercantile on the corner of Center and Main. He went on to serve the territory as its last governor, the state as its first governor, and the nation as one of Idaho's first senators.

This gathering of great hats also portrays a couple of Lemhi County's more successful entrepreneurs, c. 1910. From left to right, they are (first row) Minnie McKinney Shenon Hart and Dr. W. B. Hart; (second row) unidentified, Rose Clark McKinney, Peter McKinney, and unidentified. (Courtesy of the Bolton family.)

Ada Chase Merritt (1852–1933), mother of Allen Merritt, served as editor of *The Recorder* in Salmon, Idaho, from 1888 to 1906. Merritt and her business partner, O. W. Mintzer, promised a politically independent paper, as one editor was a Republican and the other "a Democrat without a vote, being a lady." The partnership soon fell to ruins over political differences, and Mintzer launched the *Idaho Hydraulic Gold Miner.*

Pictured here are Lou Ramey (1872–1957) and his bride, Clara Blume Ramey of Challis, on their wedding day in 1909. Lou was the first child born in the new settlement of Leesburg. His parents were John and Marjorie DeMoss Ramey. Active in local politics, Ramey served three terms as state representative for Lemhi County and helped Allen Merritt explore the regional route of Highway 93.

In 1878, William L. Mulkey (1858–1948) moved to Lemhi County. Not only did he serve two terms as Lemhi County sheriff from 1901 to 1909, he also worked as cow boss for the Shenon Land Company, running about 30,000 head of cattle. He and his wife, Idaho Pattee, daughter of Joseph and Henrietta Springer Pattee, owned and operated what is still the Mulkey Ranch at the mouth of Pratt Creek.

The Gautier family, pictured here on their Fourth of July Creek ranch around 1910, moved to Lemhi County in 1895, living in the North Fork and Gibbonsville areas. In addition to their ranch, they also owned and operated a stage stop at the mouth of Fourth of July Creek. (Courtesy of the Seth Daniels family.)

Pictured here around 1884, some of the Upper Lemhi's earliest pioneers, from left to right, are (first row) Willard Grubb, R. G. Rees, George Yearian, William Rees, Cora Yearian, Arthur Yearian, Ida Boxwell (holding a baby), Mary Gordon, Bill Pyeatt, Bob Rees, unidentified; (second row) unidentified, Andrew Clark, Cornelius Gill, Bella Rees, E. M. Yearian, Mrs. Zeph Yearian, Mrs. Thomas Pyeatt, Mrs. R. G. Rees, and Mrs. E. M Yearian. The men seated at the right are unidentified. (Courtesy of the Kenneth and Doris Yearian Collection, Lemhi County Historical Museum.)

Pictured here around 1900, from left to right, are four generations of the Andrews family: W. H. Andrews (who owned and operated a store on Main Street), N. I Andrews (who managed one of the local banks), Daisy Andrews Owens, and Daisy's baby.

Residents of Gilmore, the Andersons were part of the Pennsylvania contingent that arrived after 1909. Pictured, from left to right, are Ed Anderson, an aunt, and John Anderson. The boys' parents owned the Anderson Pool Hall in Gilmore. (Courtesy of E. Richard Benedict.)

A substantial Chinese population called Lemhi County their home in the early days and helped settle and develop the region. Pictured here are Bu Kee, a merchant in Leesburg, and his wife, Sing Chow. Bu Kee and Sing Chow remained in Leesburg until their deaths in 1928 and 1915, respectively, and are buried there. (Courtesy of the Pern family.)

This unidentified Chinese woman lived in Salmon City in the 1890s. The Chinese homes and businesses in the city were located where city hall, the library, and the museum are today. The 1870 and 1880 U.S. Census records indicate a Chinese population of 120 and 202, respectively, for Lemhi County. (Courtesy of the Shenon and Bolton families.)

Henry McCabe, a brother of Sadie Wedgewood and Mrs. Anderson of Gilmore, poses as the erstwhile miner setting out to discover his fortune. He died in Gilmore around 1920 after a fall down the stairs of the Anderson Pool Hall. Although the picture notes that he was "Mayor of Gilmore," that statement is probably not true. (Courtesy of E. Richard Benedict.)

Pictured here around 1920, Thomas, son of George and Elizabeth Stroud Yearian, and Emma Russell Yearian, who came to Lemhi County as a teacher, owned and operated what is now the Shiner Ranch at Lemhi. Two of Lemhi County's successful ranchers, it was said that she owned the sheep, but the cattle belonged to the two of them. She is now remembered as "The Sheep Queen of Idaho." (Courtesy of Jack McKinney.)

In the 1890s, Ruben and Olive Moore established a ranch on Sandy Creek, now the Steve and Diane Crofoot ranch. In the 1930s, two of their children, Roy T. and Corbin, took over the ranch operations. Five of their children, pictured from left to right, are (first row) Ted and Corbin; (second row) Ruben, Curtis, and Roy. (Courtesy of Bernice Moore Benedict.)

Arthur and Myrtle Withington were an early ranching family in Lemhi County after whom Withington Creek is named. Many of their descendants still live in the area. (Courtesy of Curtis Withington.)

Polly and Charlie Bemis, pictured at their home on Crooked Creek, were part of the Salmon River/Lemhi County community. Polly (Lalu Nathoy) arrived in the area in the 1890s and married Charlie Bemis in 1894.

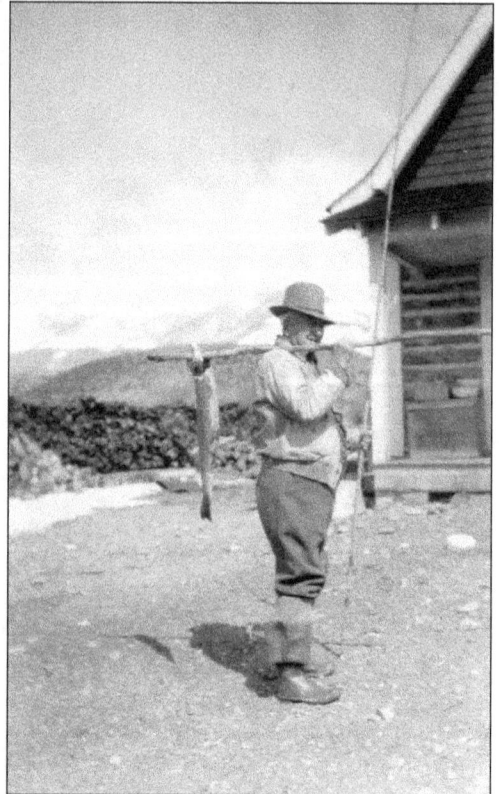

In 1887, Ernest Richard Benedict arrived in Lemhi County. He worked several jobs, including cattle buyer for a Gibbonsville butcher shop and night watchman at the AD&M Mill, to get ahead. He married Jessie Palmer in 1895 and, after a series of moves, settled on what is now the Carl Ellsworth ranch near Leadore. They had 12 children, and many of their descendants still live in the area. (Courtesy of the Benedict family.)

These residents of the Lemhi Valley near Tendoy are pictured here on a bridge across one of the creeks. Many in the photograph worked at the Lemhi Indian Agency. From left to right, they are (first row) Jack Kirkham, Edna Kadletz, Mrs. E. M. Yearian, Laura Murphey, Ethel Moore, Irene Yearian, Olive Kirkham, ? Wells, Beth Kirkham (Albertson), Bob Kirkham, and Margaret Kirkham; (second row) Mrs. Moore, Mrs. Kadletz (in the white blouse), and Margaret Kirkham (in furs and hat, kneeling); (third row) Mrs. McGee, Dr. Murphey, ? Sherman, Walter Gill, Jim Dysert, Newton Hibbs, E. M. Yearian, and unidentified.

This photograph evidently features one of the first graduating classes from the Salmon City schools. Pictured here, from left to right, are (first row) Theodora McPherson, Mame McNab, Guy Edwards, and Mame Edwards; (second row) Nellie Kirtley, Joe Williams, Hope McCaleb, Charles Kirtley, Rose Stevens, and Ettie Edwards.

95

Several of the doctors who practiced in the formative years of Lemhi County started their local practice at the Lemhi Indian Agency. Dr. George Kenney worked there in the 1870s and later moved to Salmon City. Pictured, from left to right, are (first row) Sophronia Kenney Pollard (Dr. Kenney's daughter), with Vivian Buker (Kane) on her lap; (second row) Dr. Kenney and Alice Pollard Buker.

In 1908, Dr. C. F. Hanmer opened his practice in Lemhi County in partnership with Dr. Murphey. Pictured, from left to right, are Dr. Hanmer, his son Ferguson Williams, and Dr. Hanmer's wife, Mata. F. W. "Bill" Hanmer was born in 1903 in Roosevelt, where his father served as physician for the Dewey Mining Company of Thunder Mountain. Bill married Helen Yearian, youngest daughter of Thomas and Emma.

Dr. A. F. Murphey served as Lemhi Indian Agency doctor between 1901 and 1905. In 1911, not long after establishing a practice with Dr. Hanmer, an unsatisfied patient, who was being unsuccessfully treated for an "impolite disease," shot Dr. Murphey eight times in the chest and abdomen. Afterward, the patient committed suicide; Dr. Murphey, not surprisingly, succumbed to his wounds.

Dr. W. C. Whitwell offered his services at the Lemhi Indian Agency from 1887 to 1889. He married Nora Yearian, the daughter of George and Elizabeth Yearian and sister of Thomas. Dr. Whitwell died in 1918 during the influenza epidemic, one of only two doctors treating the population of Lemhi County at that time. Pictured in this 1888 photograph at the Lemhi agency, from left to right, are (first row) Bob Stocker (boss farmer), Will Kadletz (blacksmith), and Dr. Whitwell; (second row) William Maloney and Ben Taylor (clerk).

In 1911, Dr. Owen Stratton opened his practice in Lemhi County. A native of Illinois, he attended medical school in St. Louis, Missouri, at Barnes Medical College, finishing in 1906. During World War I, he served with the Army Medical Corps but rushed back to the county when word of Dr. Whitwell's death reached him. He recounts his interesting life in *Medicine Man*, which was published by the University of Oklahoma Press.

Finishing medical school at the University of Oregon in 1887, Dr. Frank S. Wright practiced medicine in Lemhi County from 1890 to 1936—with his first five years being served at the Lemhi Agency. A Canadian by birth, "Doc" Wright became a citizen of the United States in 1889. In 1907, he married Anna Edwards, daughter of E. S. and Susan Edwards. In addition to his medical practice, he served in the state legislature.

In this *c.* 1897 photograph, Dr. Leonard, the itinerant dentist, poses on his mule, Peggie, in Salmon City. Peggie, who was commemorated in poetry in a long-lost newspaper, lived from 1894 to 1907, serving her master well.

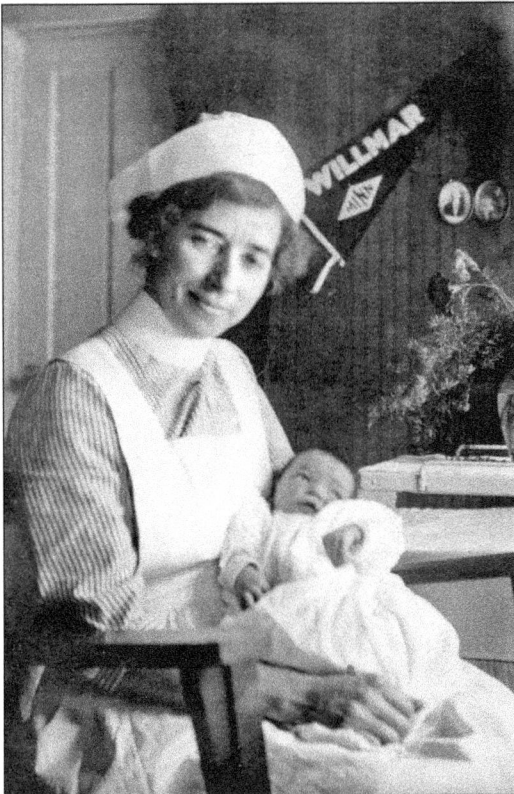

Elizabeth Clark, pictured with one of her newest patients, was a nurse at the Gilmore hospital in 1920.

Joe Bohney, one of Lemhi County's most memorable characters, is pictured here in his South St. Charles Street blacksmith shop. The shop, which stood where the Salmon Fire Department is now located, was destroyed in the aftermath of the 1962 fire at the Lemhi (Anderson) Hotel; debris falling from the brick structure obliterated his business. Bohney's first shop was in Baker, but he moved to Salmon City in 1933. (Courtesy of Rose Corum.)

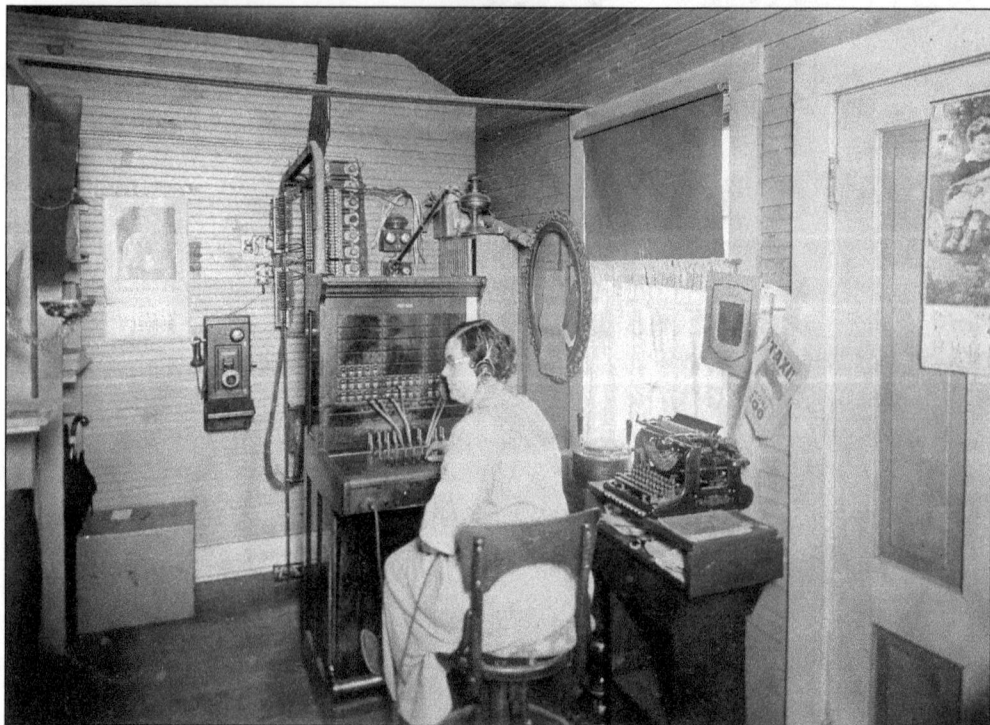

In a county as large and diverse as Lemhi, the connections were always important. Pictured operating the Leadore Telephone Exchange in 1924 is Jenny Mulkey, wife of Gus Mulkey.

Church services stimulated community spirit early in Lemhi County. This is the Methodist church in Junction in 1900; the pastor was C. Arnold Edwards.

The Methodists heard church services in Salmon City as early as 1872. By 1884, the Ladies' Church Society had raised enough money to build this church of local brick at the corner of Church Street and Main, where the Chevron station now stands. Sold in 1940, it was turned into a service station and eventually demolished.

The first Episcopal services, according to early pioneers, were offered in Salmon City as early as 1868 by Bishop Tuttle. Services were also heard at the Lemhi Indian Agency in 1902, and this church on Courthouse Drive opened its doors in 1903. It was built by Frank Pollard, a local stonemason, with stone quarried at George Shoup's quarry, west of Salmon City. (Courtesy of Patt Asplund.)

The Presbyterian church, located at the corner of Lena and McPherson Streets, was built in 1904.

The St. Charles Catholic Church, on the corner of South St. Charles Street and Hope Avenue, was built by Frank Pollard with stone from Shoup's quarry and was completed in 1911.

This first Church of Jesus Christ of Latter-day Saints in Salmon City was finished in 1929 and was located at Lillian and Shoup Streets. Although it certainly did not offer the first LDS services in the county, it served for a much longer period than the Fort Limhi Mission near Tendoy. Services were offered here until the early 1960s and a log building served as the church for members of the LDS Church in Leadore. (Courtesy of Patt Asplund.)

W. W. Schultz constructed the Lincoln School (also known as the East Side School) between 1901 and 1902 using local lumber and brick. Although sound itself, the building had been erected on swampy ground, and the resultant instability necessitated its evacuation in 1940 and its subsequent demolition in the 1950s. It stood on the current location of the junior high school football field.

This photograph of the Sandy Creek School was taken around 1900. Identified as best as possible based on the list of names on the back of the image, from left to right are (first row) unidentified and Bessie Moore (sitting); (second row) Eddie Caperon, Charlie Willie, Ivan Hughes, George McClain (against the wall), unidentified, Carrie Hughes, Lora Moore, Ida Clark, Lillian Moore, Flossie ?, Mabel McClain, Curtis Moore, Arthur McClain, and unidentified.

Pictured in this 1894 photograph of the school at North Fork, from left to right, are (first row) unidentified, unidentified, Margaret Rose (Snyder Pyeatt), Fred Rose, and Ida Anderson; (second row) Willie Noble, Fannie Noble, Frank O'Neal, unidentified, and Della Hibbs. (Courtesy of Rose Corum.)

In this photograph of the school at the mining town of Ulysses on Indian Creek, from left to right, are (first row) Billy Taylor, Frank Hibbs, Bert Buster, Harry Buster, unidentified, Jimmy Hibbs, Tolbert Bartl, Roy Layton, Rosa Buster, Rena Bartl, and Della Hibbs; (second row) Madge Buster and Nellie Bartl; (third row) Nellie Hibbs, Arnold Buster, and Myrtle Dixon.

In this 1903 class photograph at the Bridge School, from left to right, are (first row) Irvin Adams, Ralph Hagel, and Delbert Elder; (second row) John Holbrook, Russell Lee, Mary Gould, Edith Crook, and Bessie Adams; (third row) Murray Crook, Marjorie Crook, Emma Elder, Crystal Lee, Clarence Hagel, Glen Gould, Ray Cockrell, Earl Stocker, Louis Crook, Fred Hagel, Hilda Erickson, and Ella Erickson; (fourth row) Sarah Erickson, Mabel Lee, Walter Lee, Fred Currier, Clyde Holbrook, Worley Lee, and Neil Stine; (in doorway) Carl Gould and J. T. Watkins.

The Brooklyn School, completed in 1911, is still one of the finest architectural structures in Lemhi County. This photograph shows a full house, c. 1915.

This c. 1905 photograph is probably of an eighth-grade graduation, given the elegant attire of the classmates. Pictured, from left to right, are (first row) Laura Whitwell, Russell Yearian, Beth Ball, George Brown, and Claire Sharkey; (second row) Nona Vandervort, Ralph Edwards, Cassie McKinney, George Neiman, and Etta Michelson; (third row) "Hoot" Robinson, Audrey Carr, Mabel McClean, Raymond Soule, and Helen Chase.

This frame school sat on Daisy Street across from the parking lot where the original Steele Memorial Hospital (1950–2004) stood. The school held classes in the 1880s and 1890s but was abandoned due to poor insulation. It was moved to South St. Charles Street near Shoup Street. Torn down in 1929, the lumber was used to help build an apartment building.

The Tendoy School was built in 1917 and continues to serve the Tendoy area. The students, pictured here for the 1935–1936 school year, from left to right, are (first row) Aloha (Toots) Anderson, Lois Mullan, Russell Banta, Stephen Mahaffey, Elaine Langfitt, Arlene Chambers, and Ethel Barnett; (second row) Bobby Perry, Billy Perry, Viola Mullan, Mrs. Ball (Sassman), Roswell Perry, Rinaldo Jensen, and Naomi Jensen; (third row) Betty Jo Pattee, Berna Mae Barnett, Jane Pierce, Charles Barnett, Eldon Clark, and Gail Banta.

With three major rivers running through the county, the residents of the area have always been interested in fishing. Sometimes a little too interested!

At one time, sturgeon could be caught by those fishing from Island Park. Here the Gaver brothers and John Decoria are pictured with an eight-foot, eight-inch, 245-pound sturgeon. Pictured, from left to right, are John DeCoria, the sturgeon, John Gaver, and Cady Gaver.

This photograph features a community luncheon in Salmon City's downtown area near the Salmon River, c. 1925. Al Smith developed a downtown subdivision known as the "Cabbage Patch." On the east side of the river, this section had an array of cabins, two manmade mountains (Mount Shasta and Mount Rainier), and was home to many retired prospectors. Al Smith is seated at the right end of the table and is wearing a hat.

Some people were just more adventurous, as evidenced by this 1915 photograph of Cassie McKinney, Clyde Starr, Laura Whitwell (McKinney), and friends climbing toward Freeman Peak. (Courtesy of the Bolton family.)

At least some of the party made it to the top. Pictured here, from left to right, are Ralph Irvin, Carl Clark, Ormie Beers, unidentified, and Frank Bellamy, having erected a stone monument to their effort. (Courtesy of the Bolton family.)

The Salmon Band is pictured in front of the Nasholds Hotel (on the northeast corner of Center and Main Streets), c. 1900. Band members, from left to right, are (first row) Peter Marouey, Ethan Elder, Horace Ostrander, Mr. Dunlap, Mr. Parfet, unidentified, Mr. Hamilton, Joe Williams, Allen Merritt, unidentified, unidentified, Mart Tingley, Timothy Dore, unidentified, George Bryan, Fred Cowan, and Josh Billings; (second row) Jack Holbrook, Harry Goodwin, Johnny Ostrander (behind Allen Merritt), and Oscar Amonson.

The "Ladies' String Band," from left to right, are (first row) Jane Bryan Crane and Bess McNab Edwards; (second row) Jessie Peterson Matlock, Belle Kirtley, ? Phillips, Pluma Fuller, Mame McNab, Kittie Kirtley, and Irene Ramey; (third row) Gertrude Mather, ? Watkins, Kate Olds Thornhill, Rose Rood, Alpha Whitsett, Phoebe Snook Pattee, and Mabel Kadletz Rand.

Not to be outdone by its larger neighbor 65 miles away, Gilmore had its own theater and acting troupe, pictured here in 1910. From left to right, they are (first row) unidentified; (second row) W. C. Stranahan, Mrs. Dryer, and Ethel Widdowson; (third row) ? Reynolds, ? Green, Lew Britt, and ? Green.

Built in the late 1880s, the Salmon Hot Springs reached it peak in popularity in the 1930s under the Brough family's ownership. At that time, there were two pools, a dining room, two dance halls, and overnight lodging for up to 30 people.

The Salmon City Opera Society performed during the early decades of the 20th century in the Anderson Hotel, which was located at the corner of South St. Charles and Main Streets.

A significant number of the prospecting pioneers in the 1860s organized a Masonic lodge in Lemhi County on December 16, 1874. This c. 1930 photograph was taken of the Salmon Masonic Commandry No. 11, AF and AM. (Courtesy of Rose Corum.)

In this 1883 photograph of the Rocky Mountain Lodge No. 5, IOOF members are lined up along Salmon City's Main Street, a little west of their original lodge (now Kay's Hallmark). The Lemhi County Odd Fellows Association first organized in Leesburg in 1870 and relocated to Salmon City in 1875.

Eight

SCENES FROM SALMON CITY

This is one of the earliest photographs taken of Salmon City, c. 1870. The wooden toll bridge is visible in the background.

This 1910 photograph shows the steel suspension bridge crossing the Salmon River. Note the boardwalk on both sides of the street. On the north side of Main Street is the Chinese section of town, and the Fowler photograph studio is right next to the river.

Parades down Main Street have been a long-standing tradition in Salmon City. This 1898 parade features the first Lemhi County Volunteer Fire Department.

Taken from the west side of the Salmon River, this photograph offers an excellent view of Salmon City's Main Street in 1910.

Phil Shenon came to Lemhi County in the last decades of the 19th century, serving this area as hotelier, rancher, businessman, and miner. He married Minnie McKinney in 1894 and built the Shenon House, pictured here, in 1895. Before his death in 1902, he had established not only the Shenon House but the Shenon Land and Livestock Company with his brother-in-law Peter McKinney, Shenon Implement and Hardware, and the Pope-Shenon Mine. The transporting job,

featured in the foreground, necessitated connecting two teams. They hauled a "Steel Spud"—part of a dredge—to McNutt Creek for the Pacific Dredging Company. Pictured, from left to right, are (beginning directly in front of the teams) James Hockensmith, M. M. McPherson, Tommy Elder, unidentified (standing behind the horses), Joe Barrows, Al Huffman, Fred Pattee, Billy Smith, Thomas Kane, unidentified, unidentified, and Johnny McClaren.

This photograph of Salmon City's Main Street clearly depicts the city's early water system. As early as 1904, a private company supplied water to some parts of town via these wooden troughs pictured in the foreground. It was not until 1910 that the city's governing trustees decided that a more sanitary system was needed and moved to take over the water business. Created during 1911 and 1912, the Salmon Water Works offered a rudimentary filtration system—but anything would have been an improvement.

The Lemhi County Courthouse, built between 1909 and 1910, was designed by architect C. C. Rittenhouse and constructed by W. W. Schultz. Classically inspired, the courthouse features foundation blocks of granite from George Shoup's stone quarry, bricks fired by Frank Pollard, and four hand-carved Doric columns.

The hipped roof, made of steel with a terne metal covering, has an iron-ridge crest and is graced by a statue of Justice, who arrived on that roof with the help of a hay derrick. Listed on the National Historic Register, the courthouse still serves as the seat of county government.

The pioneers who came to Lemhi County were determined to create a stable community. This April 1914 photograph of the main section of Salmon City, with its brick buildings, evidences their commitment to community building and place.

Fred Viel's Economy Grocery is pictured here in 1914. It was situated near the river bridge, practically sitting on Main Street, near what is now Main Street Realty. Walter Harris, who worked for the Viels before World War II, returned to Salmon after the war, went back to work at the grocery, and eventually bought the store. Harris and his wife, Snookie, built a new store in 1956 and later joined with IGA foods.

When Salmon City celebrated the completion of the new bridge in 1926, they had an enormous parade, complete with garland arches.

The Lemhi Shoshone were invited to participate in the community bridge celebration. Horses and cars parading down Main Street offer an interesting perspective on a community still hovering

between what many consider the "Old West" and what others would see as "new."

This peaceful photograph of the Salmon River, a scow, and the tiny village that was Salmon City was taken around 1890.

BIBLIOGRAPHY

Arrington, Leonard J. *History of Idaho*. Moscow: University of Idaho Press, 1994.

Benedict, Hope Ann. "Place and Community in the Mining West: Lemhi County, Idaho, 1866–1929" Ph.D. dissertation, University of Oregon, 1996.

Benton, Jon. "Thirsty for a Water System." Unpublished.

Crowder, David. *Chief of the Lemhis*. Caldwell, Idaho: Caxton Printers, 1979.

Flanders, Robert Bruce. *Nauvoo: Kingdom on the Mississippi*. Urbana: University of Illinois Press, 1965.

Lemhi County History Book Committee. *Centennial History of Lemhi County*, Vols. I, II, and III. Salmon, ID: Lemhi County History Book Committee, 1992.

Madsen, Bringham D. *The Lemhi: Sacajawea's People*. Caldwell, Idaho: Caxton Printers, 1979.

Mann, John W. W. *Sacajawea's People: The Lemhi Shoshone and the Salmon River Country*. Lincoln: University of Nebraska Press, 2004.

Meyers, Rex. "The Implausible Gilmore and Pittsburgh." *The Colorado Rail Annual, No. 15*. Golden: Colorado Rail Museum, 1981.

Pritzker, Barry M. *A Native American Encyclopedia: History, Culture, and Peoples*. Oxford: Oxford University Press, 2000.

Ronda, James P. *Lewis and Clark Among the Indians*. Lincoln: University of Nebraska Press, 1984.

Umpleby, Joseph B. *Geology and Ore Deposits of Lemhi County, Idaho*. USGS Bulletin 528. Washington, D.C.: Department of the Interior, United States Geological Survey, 1913.

Wells, Merle. *Gold Camps and Silver Cities: Nineteenth Century Mining in Central and Southern Idaho*, 2nd edition. Moscow: Idaho Department of Lands, Bureau of Mines and Geology, 1983.

Visit us at
arcadiapublishing.com

....